T0307275

The award-winning pictures gathered in this diary have been drawn from the archives of the Wildlife Photographer of the Year competition – the international showcase for the very best nature photography. The competition is owned by the Natural History Museum, London, which prides itself on revealing and championing the diversity of life on Earth.

Wildlife Photographer of the Year is one of the most popular of the Museum's exhibitions. Visitors come not only to see breathtaking imagery, but also to understand some of the threats faced by our planet's animals and plants. Understanding and finding ways of conserving the Earth's biodiversity are at the heart of the Museum's work. This exhibition is one way to share that mission with others, encouraging us to see the environment around us with new eyes.

The Natural History Museum looks after a world-class collection of 80 million objects. It is also a leading scientific research institution, with ground-breaking projects in many countries. Over 300 scientists work at the Museum, researching the valuable collections to better understand life on Earth. Every year more than five million visitors, of all ages and levels of interest, are welcomed through the Museum's doors.

2023

JANUARY

wk	M	T	W	Th	F	S	S
52							1
1	2	3	4	5	6	7	8
2	9	10	11	12	13	14	15
3	16	17	18	19	20	21	22
4	23	24	25	26	27	28	29
5	30	31					

FEBRUARY

wk	M	T	W	Th	F	S	S
5			1	2	3	4	5
6	6	7	8	9	10	11	12
7	13	14	15	16	17	18	19
8	20	21	22	23	24	25	26
9	27	28					

MARCH

wk	M	T	W	Th	F	S	S
9			1	2	3	4	5
10	6	7	8	9	10	11	12
11	13	14	15	16	17	18	19
12	20	21	22	23	24	25	26
13	27	28	29	30	31		

APRIL

wk	M	T	W	Th	F	S	S
13						1	2
14	3	4	5	6	7	8	9
15	10	11	12	13	14	15	16
16	17	18	19	20	21	22	23
17	24	25	26	27	28	29	30

MAY

wk	M	T	W	Th	F	S	S
18	1	2	3	4	5	6	7
19	8	9	10	11	12	13	14
20	15	16	17	18	19	20	21
21	22	23	24	25	26	27	28
22	29	30	31				

JUNE

wk	M	T	W	Th	F	S	S
22				1	2	3	4
23	5	6	7	8	9	10	11
24	12	13	14	15	16	17	18
25	19	20	21	22	23	24	25
26	26	27	28	29	30		

JULY

wk	M	T	W	Th	F	S	S
26						1	2
27	3	4	5	6	7	8	9
28	10	11	12	13	14	15	16
29	17	18	19	20	21	22	23
30	24	25	26	27	28	29	30
31	31						

AUGUST

wk	M	T	W	Th	F	S	S
31		1	2	3	4	5	6
32	7	8	9	10	11	12	13
33	14	15	16	17	18	19	20
34	21	22	23	24	25	26	27
35	28	29	30	31			

SEPTEMBER

wk	M	T	W	Th	F	S	S
35					1	2	3
36	4	5	6	7	8	9	10
37	11	12	13	14	15	16	17
38	18	19	20	21	22	23	24
39	25	26	27	28	29	30	

OCTOBER

wk	M	T	W	Th	F	S	S
39							1
40	2	3	4	5	6	7	8
41	9	10	11	12	13	14	15
42	16	17	18	19	20	21	22
43	23	24	25	26	27	28	29
44	30	31					

NOVEMBER

wk	M	T	W	Th	F	S	S
44			1	2	3	4	5
45	6	7	8	9	10	11	12
46	13	14	15	16	17	18	19
47	20	21	22	23	24	25	26
48	27	28	29	30			

DECEMBER

wk	M	T	W	Th	F	S	S
48					1	2	3
49	4	5	6	7	8	9	10
50	11	12	13	14	15	16	17
51	18	19	20	21	22	23	24
52	25	26	27	28	29	30	31

2024

JANUARY

wk	M	T	W	Th	F	S	S
1	1	2	3	4	5	6	7
2	8	9	10	11	12	13	14
3	15	16	17	18	19	20	21
4	22	23	24	25	26	27	28
5	29	30	31				

FEBRUARY

wk	M	T	W	Th	F	S	S
5				1	2	3	4
6	5	6	7	8	9	10	11
7	12	13	14	15	16	17	18
8	19	20	21	22	23	24	25
9	26	27	28	29			

MARCH

wk	M	T	W	Th	F	S	S
9					1	2	3
10	4	5	6	7	8	9	10
11	11	12	13	14	15	16	17
12	18	19	20	21	22	23	24
13	25	26	27	28	29	30	31

APRIL

wk	M	T	W	Th	F	S	S
14	1	2	3	4	5	6	7
15	8	9	10	11	12	13	14
16	15	16	17	18	19	20	21
17	22	23	24	25	26	27	28
18	29	30					

MAY

wk	M	T	W	Th	F	S	S
18			1	2	3	4	5
19	6	7	8	9	10	11	12
20	13	14	15	16	17	18	19
21	20	21	22	23	24	25	26
22	27	28	29	30	31		

JUNE

wk	M	T	W	Th	F	S	S
22						1	2
23	3	4	5	6	7	8	9
24	10	11	12	13	14	15	16
25	17	18	19	20	21	22	23
26	24	25	26	27	28	29	30

JULY

wk	M	T	W	Th	F	S	S
27	1	2	3	4	5	6	7
28	8	9	10	11	12	13	14
29	15	16	17	18	19	20	21
30	22	23	24	25	26	27	28
31	29	30	31				

AUGUST

wk	M	T	W	Th	F	S	S
31				1	2	3	4
32	5	6	7	8	9	10	11
33	12	13	14	15	16	17	18
34	19	20	21	22	23	24	25
35	26	27	28	29	30	31	

SEPTEMBER

wk	M	T	W	Th	F	S	S
35							1
36	2	3	4	5	6	7	8
37	9	10	11	12	13	14	15
38	16	17	18	19	20	21	22
39	23	24	25	26	27	28	29
40	30						

OCTOBER

wk	M	T	W	Th	F	S	S
40		1	2	3	4	5	6
41	7	8	9	10	11	12	13
42	14	15	16	17	18	19	20
43	21	22	23	24	25	26	27
44	28	29	30	31			

NOVEMBER

wk	M	T	W	Th	F	S	S
44					1	2	3
45	4	5	6	7	8	9	10
46	11	12	13	14	15	16	17
47	18	19	20	21	22	23	24
48	25	26	27	28	29	30	

DECEMBER

wk	M	T	W	Th	F	S	S
48							1
49	2	3	4	5	6	7	8
50	9	10	11	12	13	14	15
51	16	17	18	19	20	21	22
52	23	24	25	26	27	28	29
1	30	31					

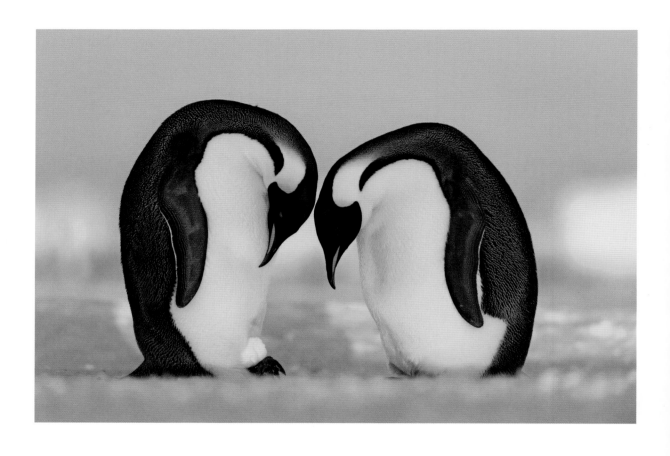

December – January

26 Monday   Boxing Day, holiday (Christian)

27 Tuesday   Christmas Day, holiday (Christian)

28 Wednesday

29 Thursday

30 Friday

31 Saturday   New Year's Eve
Hogmanay (Scotland)

1 Sunday   New Year's Day

Training session by Stefan Christmann
When Stefan came across this penguin couple in Atka Bay, Antarctica, he was surprised, as it was too early in the season for egg-laying. Upon closer inspection he discovered the egg was a snowball. Perhaps the diligent couple were practising egg transfer in preparation for when their real egg arrived.

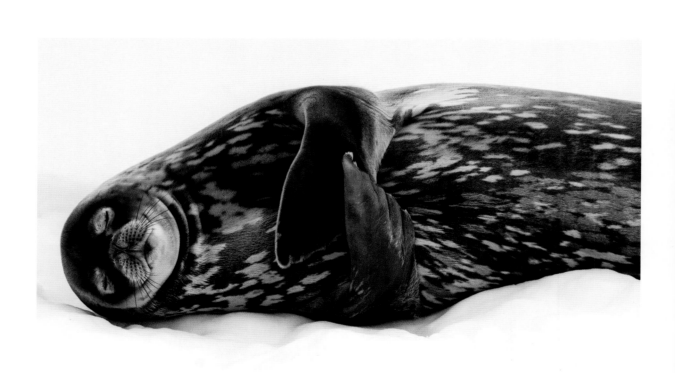

January

2 Monday

3 Tuesday

4 Wednesday

5 Thursday

6 Friday

Epiphany (Christian)

7 Saturday

8 Sunday

Sleeping like a Weddell by Ralf Schneider
Hugging its flippers tight to its body, this Weddell seal off Larsen Harbour,
South Georgia, appeared to fall into a deep sleep. From an inflatable boat,
Ralf tightly framed the seal, and using the icy white backdrop and soft light
from the overcast sky he mimicked the effect of a studio portrait.

9 Monday

10 Tuesday

11 Wednesday

12 Thursday

13 Friday

14 Saturday

15 Sunday

Family get-together by Michael Schober
Marmots have become accustomed to the presence of humans in Hohe
Tauern National Park, Austria, and allow people to observe and photograph
them at close range. This behaviour is beneficial for the marmots, as human
company deters predators such as golden eagles.

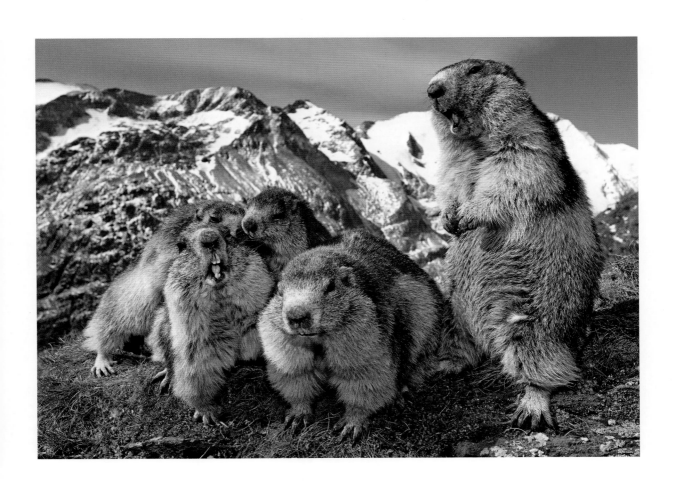

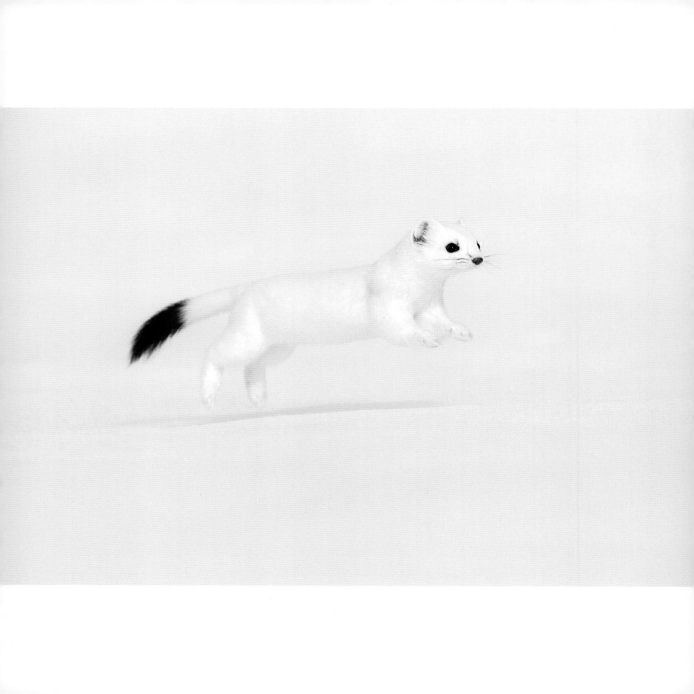

January

WEEK 3

16 Monday Martin Luther King Day (USA)

17 Tuesday

18 Wednesday

19 Thursday

20 Friday

21 Saturday

22 Sunday Chinese New Year (Year of the Rabbit)

Snow hunting by Jérémie Villet
Camouflaged in its white winter coat, a stoat bounds over a snowy field hunting for voles in the Jura Mountains of eastern France. The land owner was using poison to kill the voles, but Jérémie persuaded him, through his photographs, to let these beautiful little predators do the work.

January

23 Monday

24 Tuesday

25 Wednesday   Burns Night (Scotland)

26 Thursday   Australia Day

27 Friday

28 Saturday

29 Sunday

Inquisitive by Audun Rikardsen
From a hide on the coast of northern Norway, it took Audun three years
of planning to capture this majestic bird of prey in its coastal environment.
After some time, the golden eagle became curious of the camera and
seemed to like being in the spotlight.

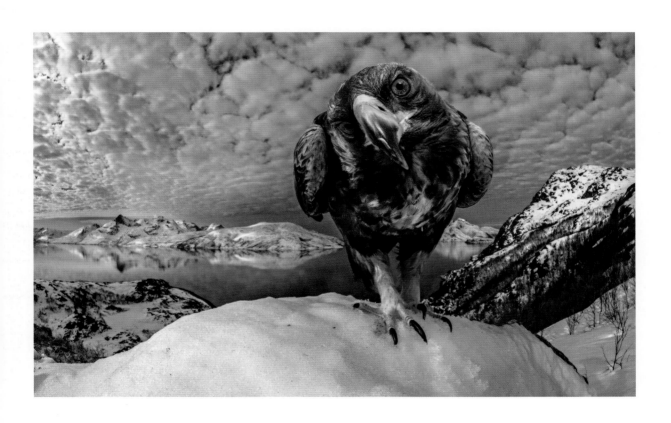

January – February

30 Monday

31 Tuesday

1 Wednesday

2 Thursday

3 Friday

4 Saturday

5 Sunday

Snow exposure by Max Waugh
In a winter whiteout in Yellowstone National Park, a lone American bison
stands weathering the silent snowstorm. Slowing his shutter speed to blur
the snow, Max created an abstract image that combines the stillness of
the animal with the movement of the snowfall.

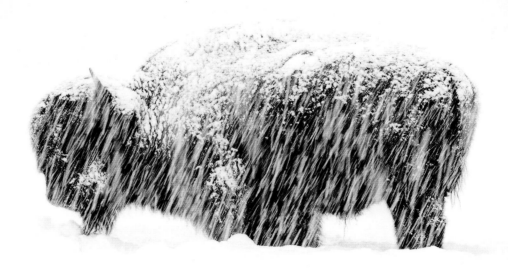

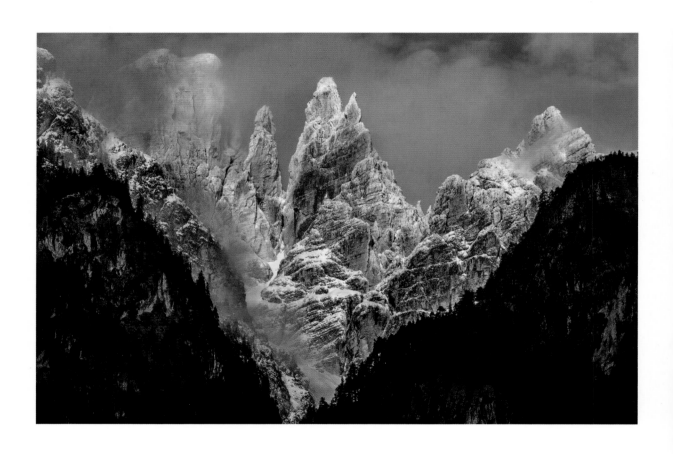

6 Monday
_____

7 Tuesday
_____

8 Wednesday
_____

9 Thursday
_____

10 Friday
_____

11 Saturday	12 Sunday

The frozen spires by Roberto Zanette
Roberto has photographed the dramatic Dolomite massif of Croda dei Toni
in the Italian Alps, many times. On this particular morning, when the clouds
cleared, the scene appeared very different – snow had settled on the vertical
faces and, most unusually, on several of the downward-facing surfaces.

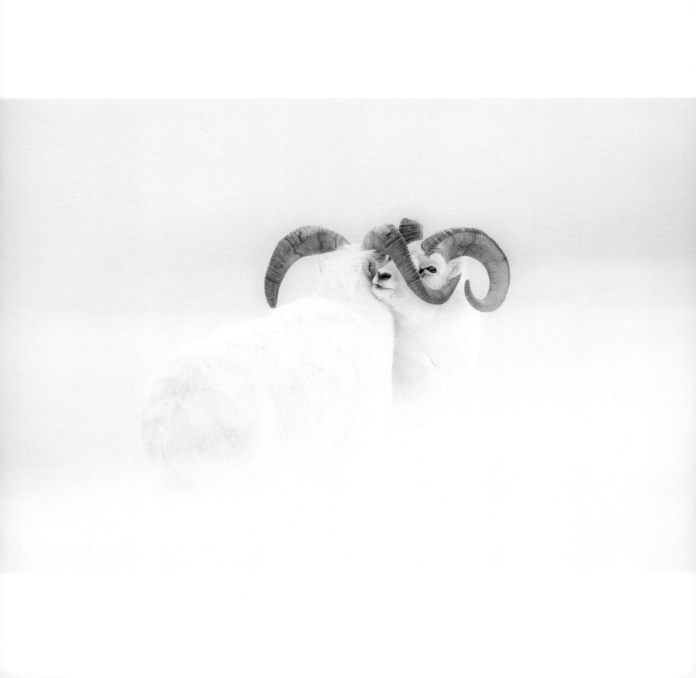

---

13 Monday

---

14 Tuesday

Valentine's Day

---

15 Wednesday

---

16 Thursday

---

17 Friday

---

18 Saturday

19 Sunday

Frozen moment by Jérémie Villet
On a steep ridge, two male Dall's sheep attempted to duel for mating rights, but a heavy blizzard forced them into a truce. Lying in the snow, Jérémie was also battling with the brutal weather in Yukon, Canada – his fingers were frozen and the ferocious wind was making it difficult to hold his lens steady.

February

20 Monday   George Washington's Birthday (USA)

21 Tuesday   Shrove Tuesday, Pancake Day (Christian)

22 Wednesday   Ash Wednesday (Christian)

23 Thursday

24 Friday

25 Saturday

26 Sunday

The humpback calf by Wayne Osborn
Wayne spotted this male humpback calf and its mother while diving off the
Vava'u Island group in the Kingdom of Tonga. The calf kept a curious eye
on Wayne as it twisted and turned. Periodically it returned to its mother to
suckle, who was relaxed and motionless 20 m (65 ft) below.

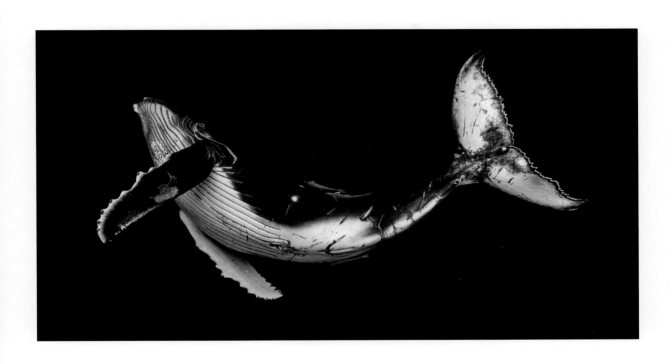

---

27 Monday

---

28 Tuesday

---

1 Wednesday   St David's Day (Wales)

---

2 Thursday

---

3 Friday

---

4 Saturday | 5 Sunday

Matching outfits by Michel Zoghzoghi
Michel was in the Pantanal, Brazil, photographing jaguars. One afternoon, as he was on the Três Irmãos River, a mother and her cub crossed right in front of his boat. He watched, mesmerized, as they left the water carrying an anaconda in their mouths with a very similar pattern to their own.

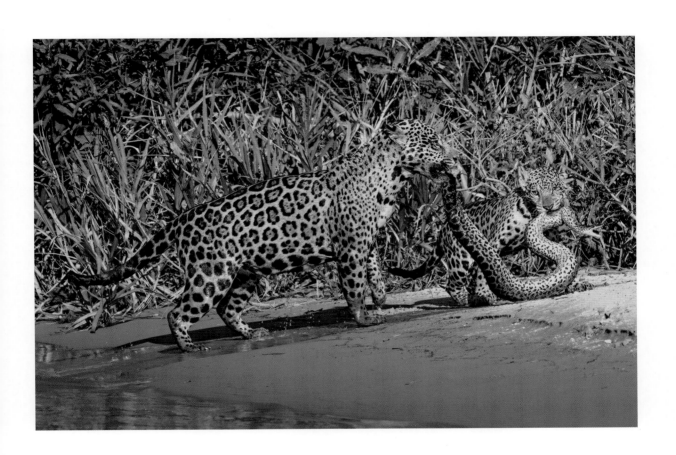

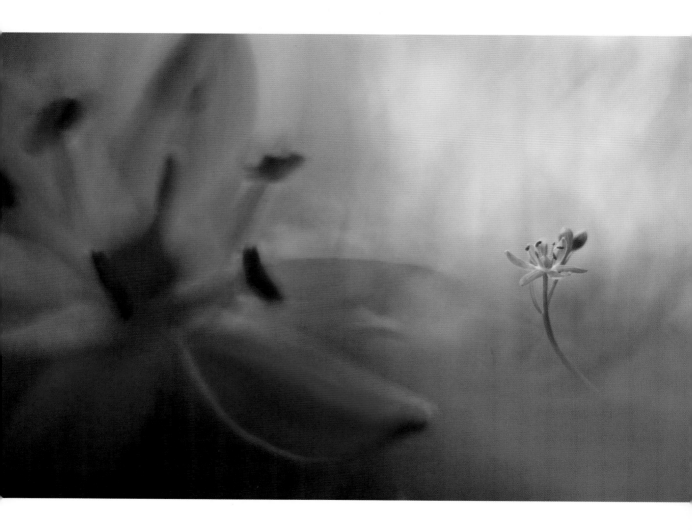

March

6 Monday

7 Tuesday

8 Wednesday

9 Thursday

10 Friday

11 Saturday

12 Sunday

Spring vision by Imre Potyó
The delicate woodland scillas flowering for only a week on the God
floodplain in Hungary's Danube-Ipoly National Park are to Imre, the essence
of early spring. In this double-exposure image, he shot the petals of one
bloom close up and then focused on another flower.

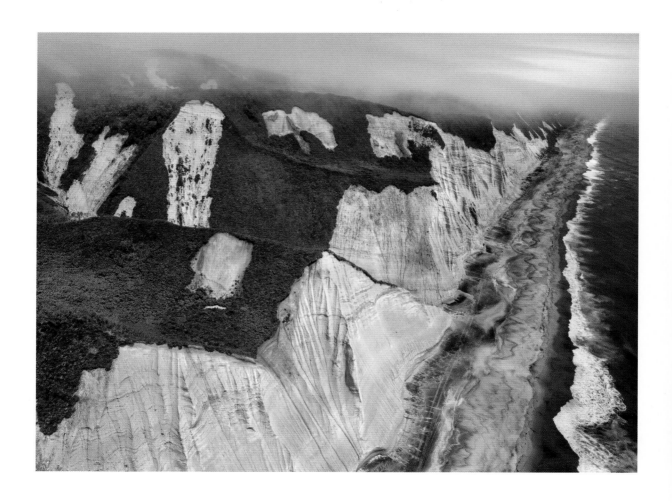

---

13 Monday

---

14 Tuesday

---

15 Wednesday

---

16 Thursday

---

17 Friday   St Patrick's Day, holiday (Ireland)

---

18 Saturday	**19** Sunday Mothering Sunday

The white cliffs of Iturup by Alexey Kharitonov
Flying his drone along the remote island coastline of Iturup, Russia, Alexey
was awestruck by the images on his screen – a vast beach of volcanic sand
and pure-white cliffs covered in a carpet of green Kuril bamboo. He wanted
to capture the 'beauty and uniqueness' of the island's wild landscape.

March

---

20 Monday
Spring Equinox

---

21 Tuesday

---

22 Wednesday
Ramadan (Islamic)
begins in the evening

---

23 Thursday

---

24 Friday

---

25 Saturday

26 Sunday
British Summertime begins,
clocks go forward

Dinner for one by Ripan Biswas
For Ripan, the real lure of the Buxa Tiger Reserve, India, is not big cats but insects. On this afternoon, he became fascinated by a golden shoot fly, just 6 mm (¼ in) long, feeding on liquid in an empty snail shell. Switching his lens to macro he was able to capture the fly's features in remarkable detail.

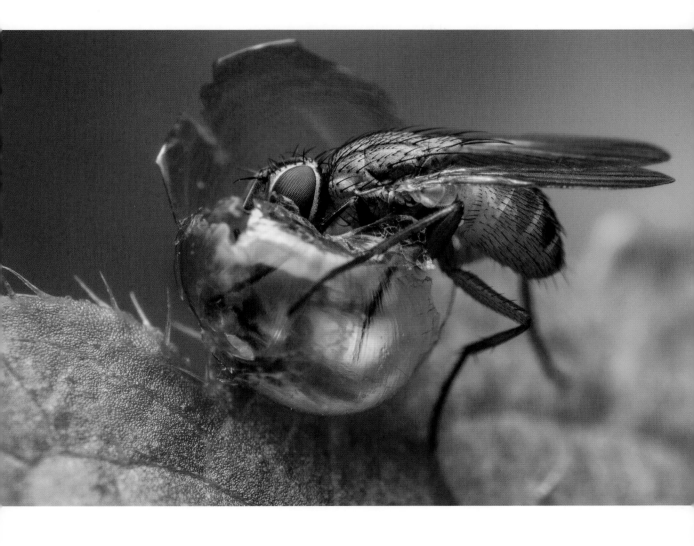

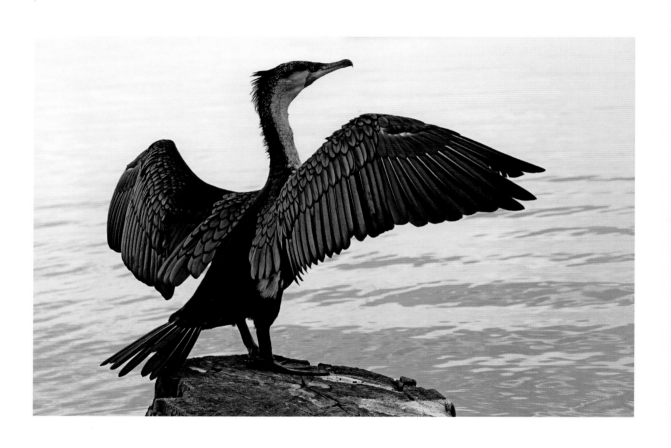

27 Monday

28 Tuesday

29 Wednesday

30 Thursday

31 Friday

1 Saturday   April Fools' Day

2 Sunday   Palm Sunday (Christian)

Great cormorant dry-off by Soumil Rathi
The white-breasted cormorant was warming up in the sun with its wings
outstretched on an island in Kenya's Lake Naivasha. In a constantly swaying
rowing boat, Soumil was pleased to get a sharp image highlighting its glossy
bronze upper-wing feathers and distinctive green eye.

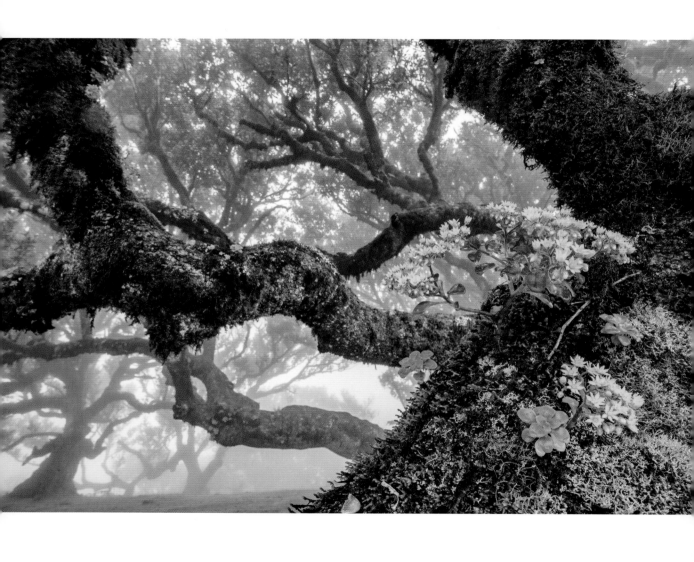

3 Monday

4 Tuesday

5 Wednesday

First day of Passover (Jewish)
begins in the evening

6 Thursday

Maundy Thursday (Christian)

7 Friday

Good Friday, holiday (Christian)

8 Saturday

9 Sunday

Easter Sunday (Christian)

Forest refuge by Uge Fuertes Sanz
This native stonecrop adds a splash of yellow to a vast tilo tree in the fog-
ridden Fanal Forest, Madeira. 'Everywhere I looked there were magical forms,'
says Uge. When the fog cleared enough to add just a touch of mystery, he
held his camera aloft, shooting blindly, until he captured the perfect image.

April

10 Monday

Easter Monday, holiday (Christian)

11 Tuesday

12 Wednesday

13 Thursday

Last day of Passover (Jewish)
ends in the evening

14 Friday

15 Saturday

16 Sunday

Night rider by Wayne Jones
A juvenile paper nautilus – a species of pelagic octopus – rides atop a small
jellyfish in Janao Bay near Anilao in the Philippines. Drawn to the electric
green tentacles of the jellyfish against the inky blackness, it wasn't until
Wayne moved closer that he spotted the hitchhiker.

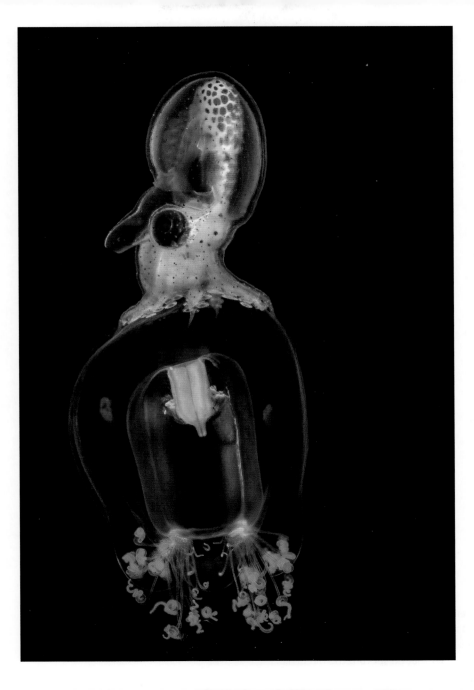

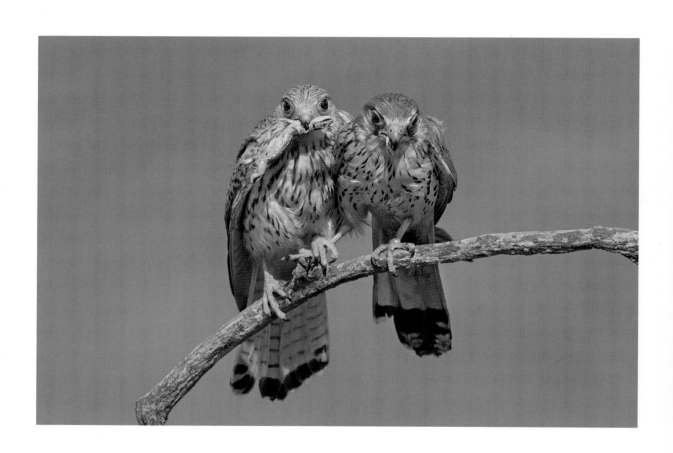

April

17 Monday

18 Tuesday

19 Wednesday

20 Thursday

Ramadan (Islamic)
ends in the evening

21 Friday

22 Saturday

23 Sunday

St George's Day (England)

A suitable gift by Marco Valentini
Marco was in Hortobágyi National Park, Hungary, when he spotted these
kestrels displaying typical courtship behaviour. Here the female has just
received an offering of a young green lizard from her suitor and, in this
touching moment, she tenderly took hold of his claw.

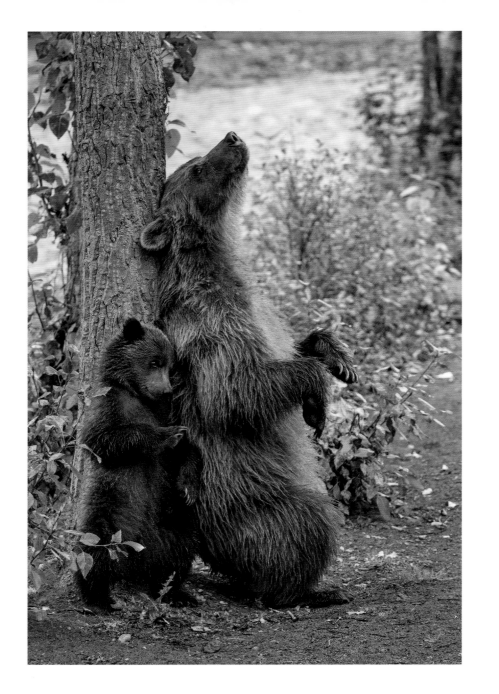

24 Monday

25 Tuesday

26 Wednesday

27 Thursday

28 Friday

29 Saturday

30 Sunday

Mother knows best by Marion Vollborn
While on a bear watching trip to the Nakina River in British Columbia,
Canada, Marion spotted a grizzly bear and her young cub approaching a
tree. The mother bear started to rub against the tree trunk and was followed
shortly by the cub, imitating its mother.

May

1 Monday	May Day holiday (UK, Scotland)

2 Tuesday

3 Wednesday

4 Thursday

5 Friday

6 Saturday	**7 Sunday**

The freshwater forest by Michel Roggo
Stems of Eurasian water milfoil reach for the sky from the bed of Lake
Neuchatel, Switzerland. Michel has photographed freshwater regions
worldwide, but this was his first dive in the lake nearest to his home. To his
amazement he discovered an 'underwater jungle with an endless view'.

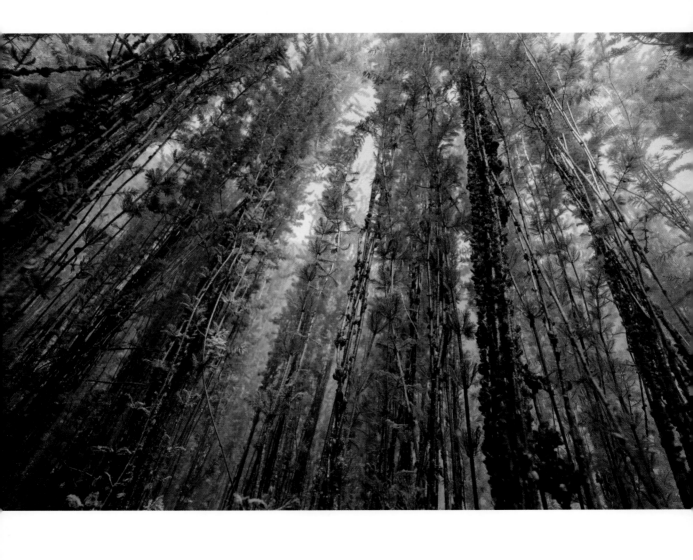

May

8 Monday

9 Tuesday

10 Wednesday

11 Thursday

12 Friday

13 Saturday

14 Sunday

Dinner duty by Tommy Pedersen
Perched on a tall birch stump in Arvika, western Sweden, a male great grey
owl delivers a meal to his offspring. The precious chick, nestled safely under
the wing of its mother, is the only one left of a clutch of three. Using a wide
aperture in the evening light, Tommy captured this tender family moment.

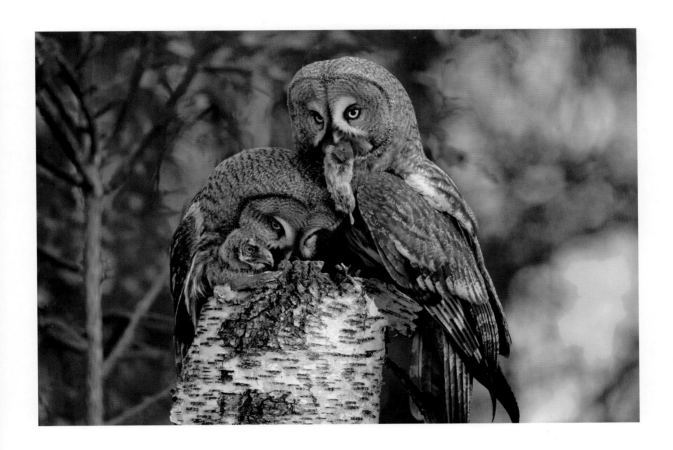

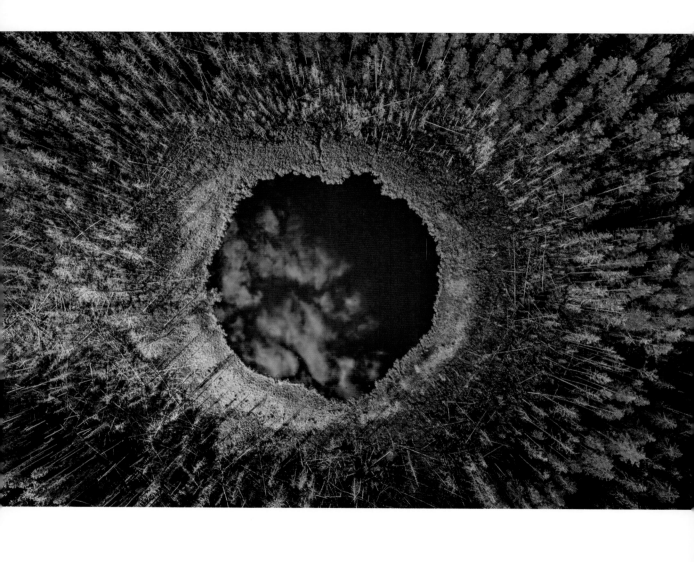

May

---

15 Monday

---

16 Tuesday

---

17 Wednesday

---

18 Thursday   Ascension Day (Christian)

---

19 Friday

---

20 Saturday	21 Sunday

Sky hole by Sven Zacek
After many years exploring Estonia's Karula National Park, Sven discovered
this extraordinary circular lake deep in the forest. Positioning his drone
directly above it, he waited for the sun to emerge, and captured the
reflection of the sky in the lake's mirrored surface.

May

22 Monday

23 Tuesday

24 Wednesday

25 Thursday

26 Friday

27 Saturday

28 Sunday   Whitsun (Christian)

Trustful by Ingo Arndt
Ingo has followed the pumas of Torres del Paine National Park, in Patagonia,
Chile, for over two years, and they are used to his presence. This female
was so at ease, she fell asleep nearby. On wakening, she glanced at him in a
familiar way, and he captured this portrait of a completely relaxed puma.

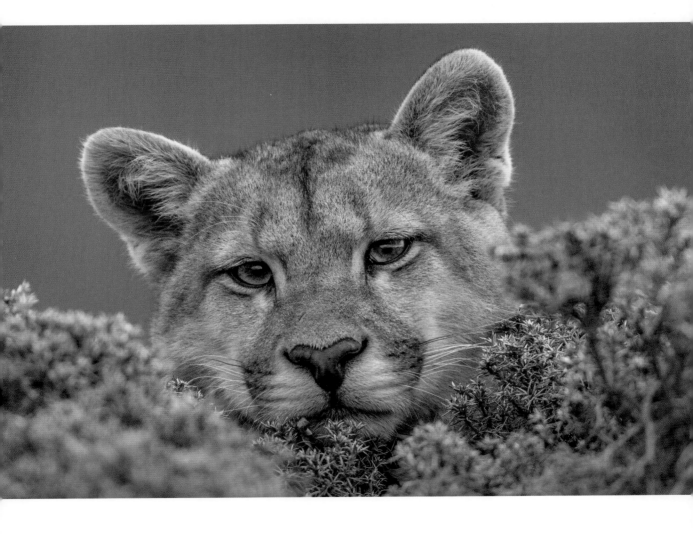

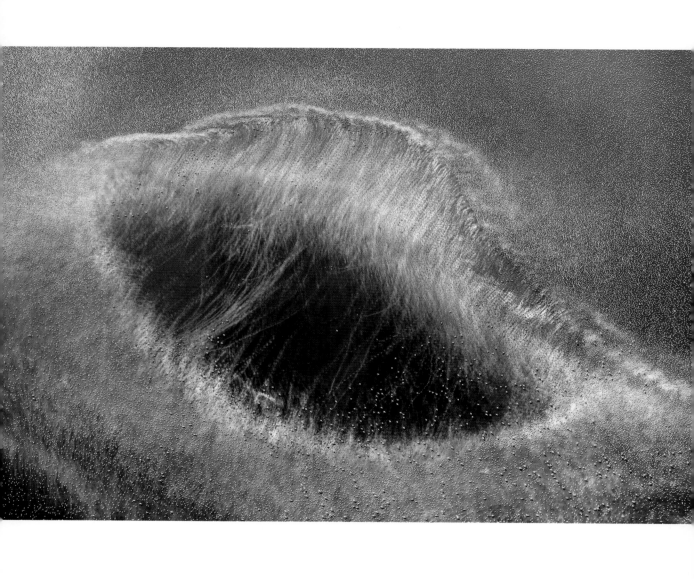

May – June

29 Monday   Spring holiday (UK, Scotland)

30 Tuesday

31 Wednesday

1 Thursday

2 Friday

3 Saturday   **4 Sunday**   Trinity Sunday (Christian)

Lake of a million birds by Paul Mckenzie
Flying high over Kenya's Lake Logipi in a light aircraft, Paul concentrated on a
group of more than 100,000 lesser and greater flamingos. Leaning out of an
open door, he used a fast shutter speed to counter the turbulence, capturing
the patterns of both the pink birds and their filter-feeding trails in the silt.

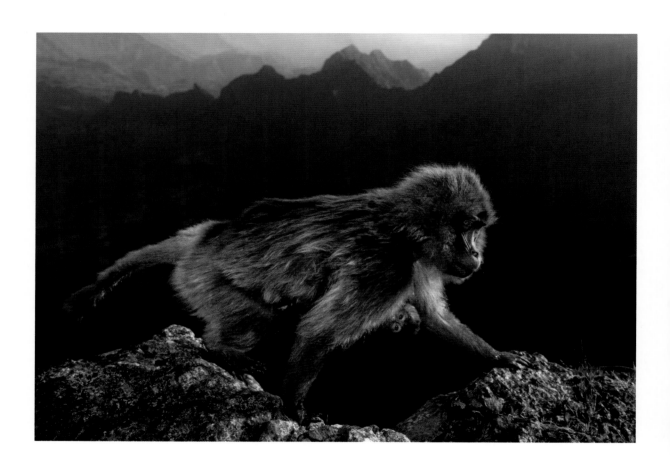

June

---

5 Monday
June holiday (Republic of Ireland)

---

6 Tuesday

---

7 Wednesday

---

8 Thursday
Corpus Christi (Christian)

---

9 Friday

---

10 Saturday Queen Elizabeth II's birthday | **11 Sunday**

Early riser by Riccardo Marchegiani
Riccardo could not believe his luck when, at first light, this female gelada, with a tiny infant clinging to her, climbed over the cliff edge close to where he was. Shooting with a low flash he highlighted her rich brown fur against the still-dark mountain range in Ethiopia's Simien Mountains National Park.

12 Monday

13 Tuesday

14 Wednesday

15 Thursday

16 Friday

17 Saturday

18 Sunday   Father's Day

Humming surprise by Thomas Easterbrook
On a warm summer's evening in France, Thomas heard the fast-beating
wings of a hummingbird hawkmoth. It was hovering in front of a *Salvia* plant,
siphoning up nectar with its long proboscis, and moving quickly from flower
to flower, making it a challenge to capture.

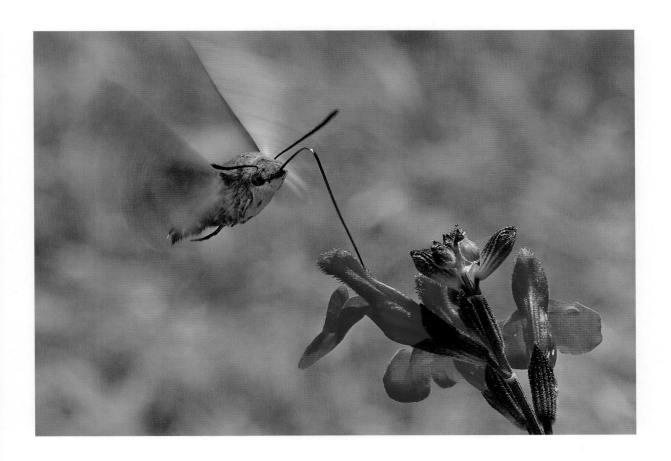

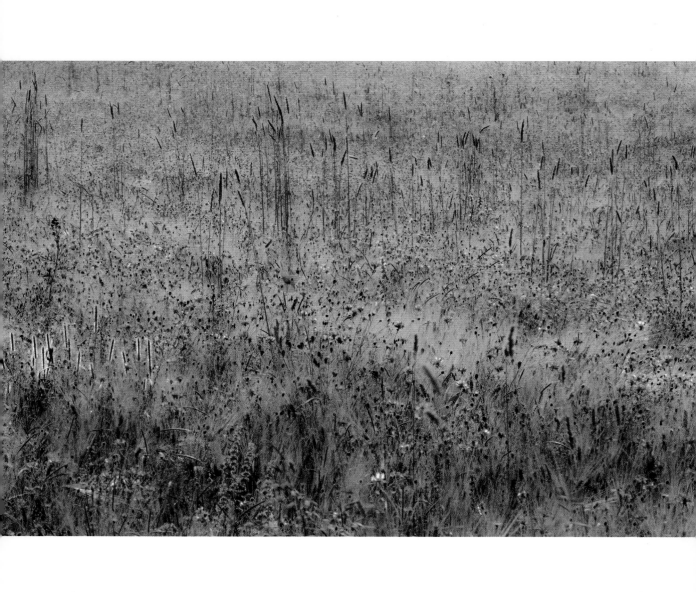

June

19 Monday

20 Tuesday

21 Wednesday   Summer Solstice

22 Thursday

23 Friday

24 Saturday   **25 Sunday**

Summer cornfield by Joël Brunet
The cornflower and the poppy are familiar European symbols of remembrance
for war veterans but a vibrant summer cornfield where these species thrive
naturally has become a rare sight. Joël was moved by the scarlet poppies in an
expanse of blue and gold glimmering in the morning light.

June – July

26 Monday

27 Tuesday

28 Wednesday

29 Thursday

30 Friday

1 Saturday   Canada Day | **2 Sunday**

A bite to eat by Jaime Culebras
Jaime was in the Veragua Rainforest Reserve, Costa Rica, when he spotted
a northern cat-eyed snake slowly moving towards a gathering of frogs.
Approaching cautiously, he waited several hours for the snake to make its
choice. In a lightning strike, it finally grabbed a male hourglass treefrog.

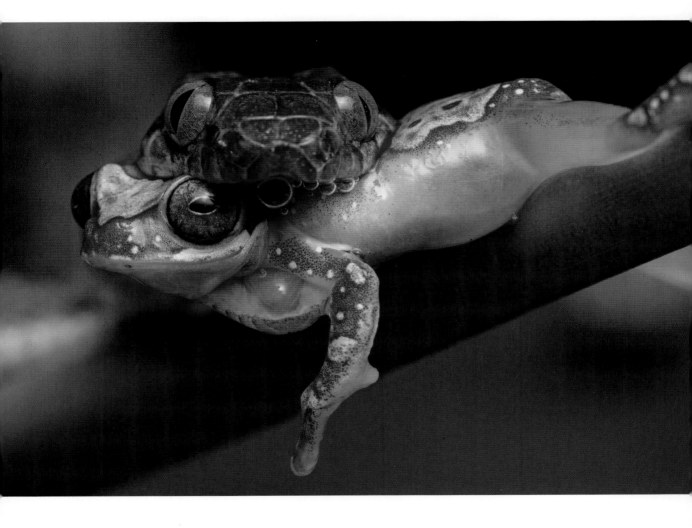

3 Monday

4 Tuesday

Independence Day (USA)

5 Wednesday

6 Thursday

7 Friday

8 Saturday

9 Sunday

A swirl of rays by Duncan Murrell
Duncan has been diving in Honda Bay in the Philippine island province of
Palawan for more than a decade. In a courtship ballet two male spinetail
devil rays vied for the attention of a female. Duncan, who was snorkelling
above, instinctively captured this seldom-seen behaviour.

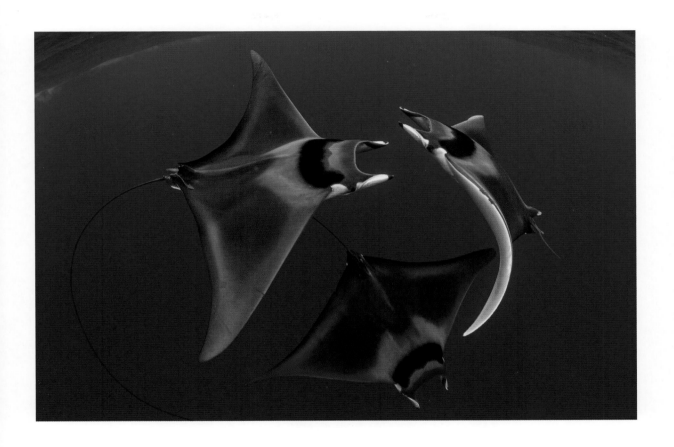

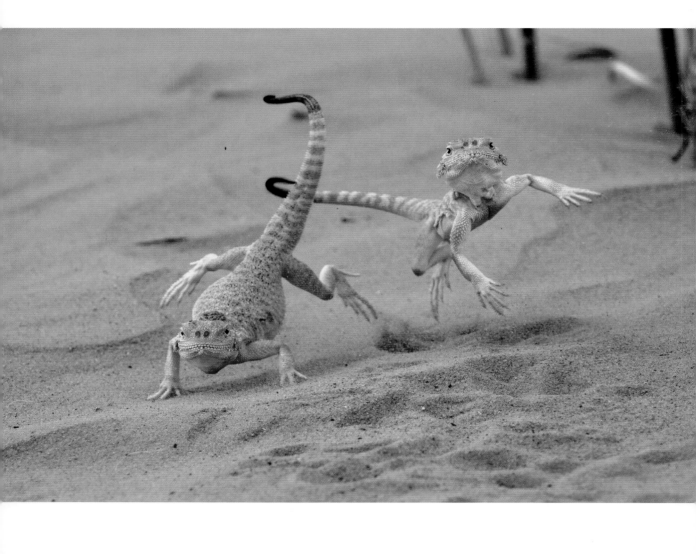

10 Monday

11 Tuesday

12 Wednesday

Battle of the Boyne,
holiday (Northern Ireland)

13 Thursday

14 Friday

15 Saturday

St Swithin's Day (Christian)

16 Sunday

War dance by Victor Tyakht
In the Republic of Kalmykia, southwestern Russia, two rival toad-headed
agamas run and jump alongside one another in an energetic display
designed to warn off the weaker opponent. These lizards are extremely
territorial and fiercely protect their domain.

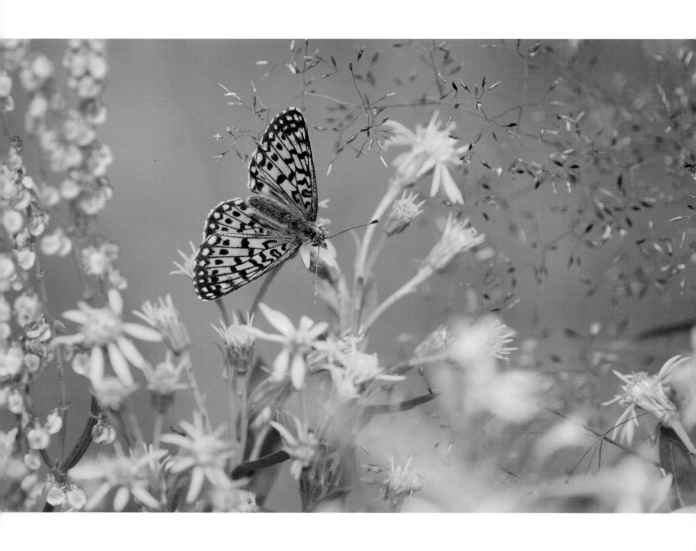

July

---

17 Monday

---

18 Tuesday

---

19 Wednesday

---

20 Thursday

---

21 Friday

---

22 Saturday	23 Sunday

Meadow beauty by Alfons Lilja
On a warm summer's day in a meadow by the sea in northeast Sweden,
Alfons spotted this small pearl-bordered fritillary flying close to the ground.
It paused to drink nectar from a clump of goldenrods and he was delighted
that it stayed still long enough for him to capture this shot.

July

---

24 Monday

---

25 Tuesday

---

26 Wednesday

---

27 Thursday

---

28 Friday

---

29 Saturday

30 Sunday

A pulsing sea by David Doubilet
A school of red tooth triggerfish form a cloud of silhouettes above convict
blennies in the coral ecosystem of the Verde Island Passage, Philippines. The
Passage, a strait that separates the islands of Luzon and Mindoro, is one of
the most productive marine ecosystems in the world.

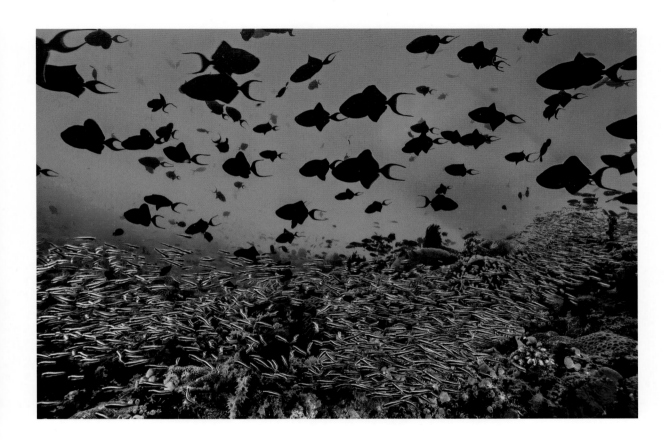

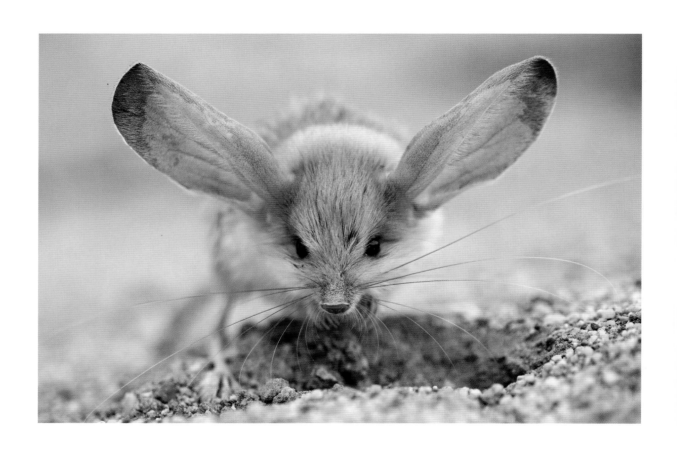

July – August

31 Monday

1 Tuesday

2 Wednesday

3 Thursday

4 Friday

5 Saturday

6 Sunday

Big ears by Valeriy Maleev
Valeriy was on a summer expedition to the Mongolian part of the Gobi
Desert when he happened upon a long-eared jerboa. As blood moves
through the ears of these usually nocturnal animals, excess heat dissipates
across the skin and so the jerboa is able to stay cool.

August

7 Monday   Summer holiday (Scotland, Republic of Ireland)

8 Tuesday

9 Wednesday

10 Thursday

11 Friday

12 Saturday   **13 Sunday**

Bee line by Frank Deschandol
As evening fell in Morocco's Atlas Mountains, bees buzzed in the long grass,
and to Frank's delight, were settling down in little rows along the grass stems.
These were solitary bees, probably males, gathering for the night in suitable
resting places while the females occupied nearby underground nests.

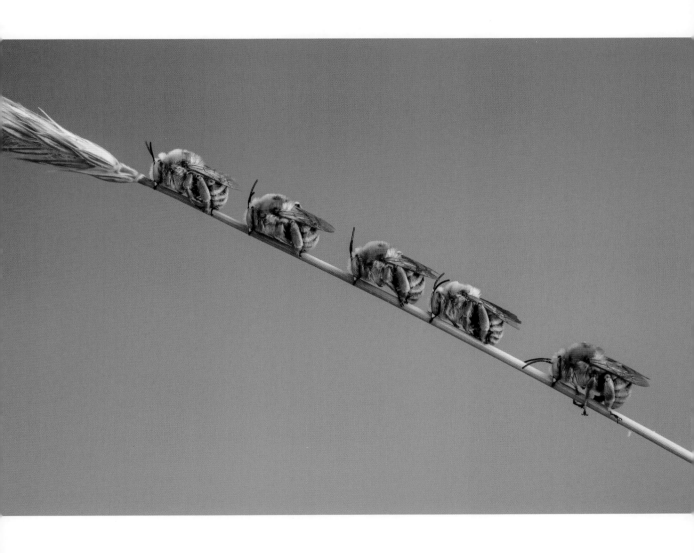

August

14 Monday

15 Tuesday

16 Wednesday

17 Thursday

18 Friday

19 Saturday

20 Sunday

Beak to beak by Claudio Contreras Koob
Ría Lagartos Biosphere Reserve in the state of Yucatán is home to Mexico's
largest flock of Caribbean flamingos. This chick is less than five days old
– it will stay in its nest less than a week before it joins a crèche of other
youngsters who wander around the colony searching for food.

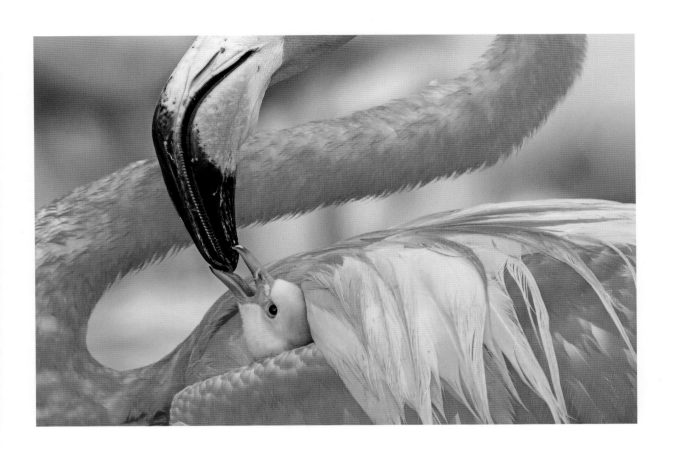

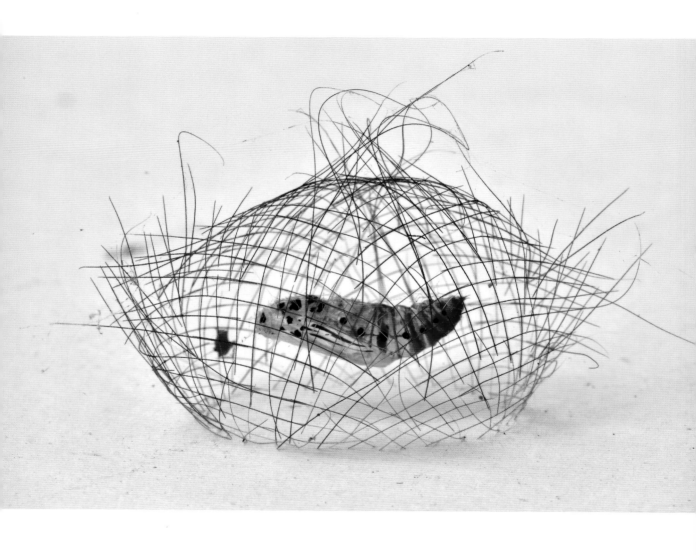

August

21 Monday

22 Tuesday

23 Wednesday

24 Thursday

25 Friday

26 Saturday

27 Sunday

The hair-net cocoon by Minghui Yuan
Minghui framed this *Cyana* moth pupa in Xishuangbanna Tropical Botanical
Garden, southwest China. It had used its long, hair-like setae to weave a
delicate cage-like cocoon, inside which it would pupate. Hard to spot in
more natural habitats, this one stood out against its backdrop in a WC.

August – September

---

28 Monday   Summer holiday (UK, excluding Scotland)

---

29 Tuesday

---

30 Wednesday

---

31 Thursday

---

1 Friday

---

2 Saturday	**3 Sunday**

The charm of Ruthy by Ariel Fields
Every night a female striped hyena, locally known as Ruthy, enters the city of
Modi'in-Maccabim-Re'ut, central Israel, to forage for scraps. Twice she has
been captured and relocated, and each time she has returned to the city. At
dusk Ariel spotted her dozing – ears alert – ahead of a night scavenging.

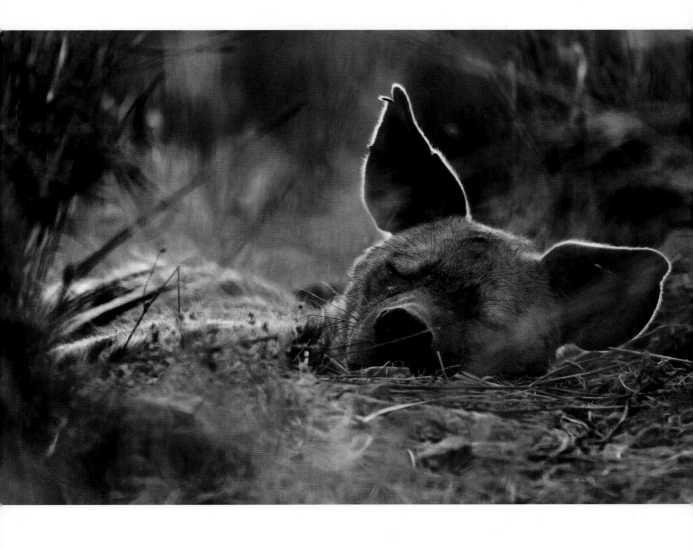

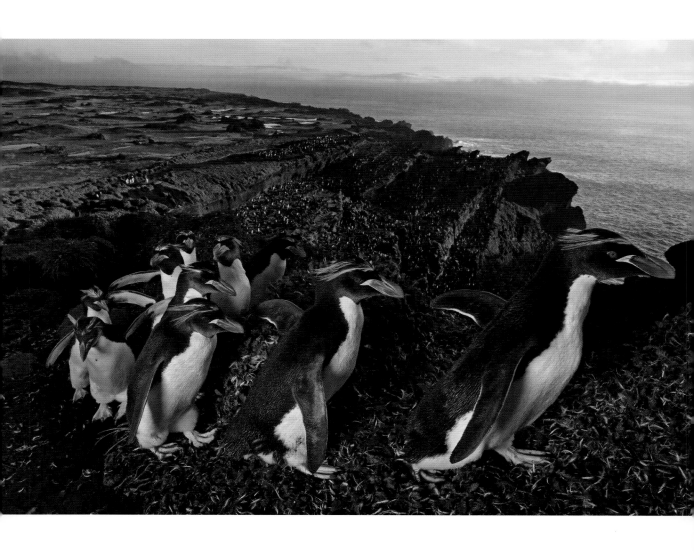

September

4 Monday

5 Tuesday

6 Wednesday

7 Thursday

8 Friday

9 Saturday

10 Sunday

The plumage parade by Thomas P Peschak
Dapper in their stylish yellow head feathers, these macaroni penguins waddle
up an old volcano crater to their roosting terrace on the remote South
African island of Marion. Thomas had just a few hours with them before a
storm engulfed the coast and most of them headed back out to sea.

11 Monday

12 Tuesday

13 Wednesday

14 Thursday

15 Friday

Rosh Hashanah, Jewish New Year
begins in the evening

16 Saturday

17 Sunday

Rosh Hashanah, Jewish New Year
ends in the evening

Portrait of a mother by Ingo Arndt
The pumas of the Torres del Paine region of Patagonia, Chile, are elusive, roaming over large territories. Tracking them on foot was hard work but Ingo gradually gained the trust of this female over two and a half years, and he was rewarded with this intimate portrait of her and her five-month-old cubs.

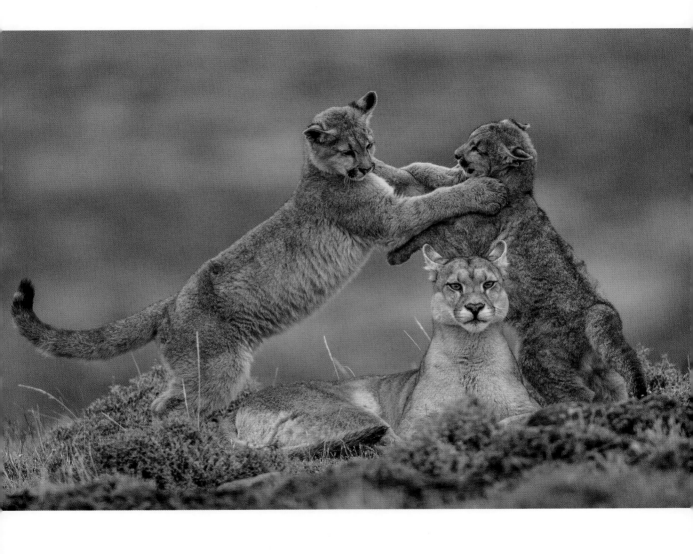

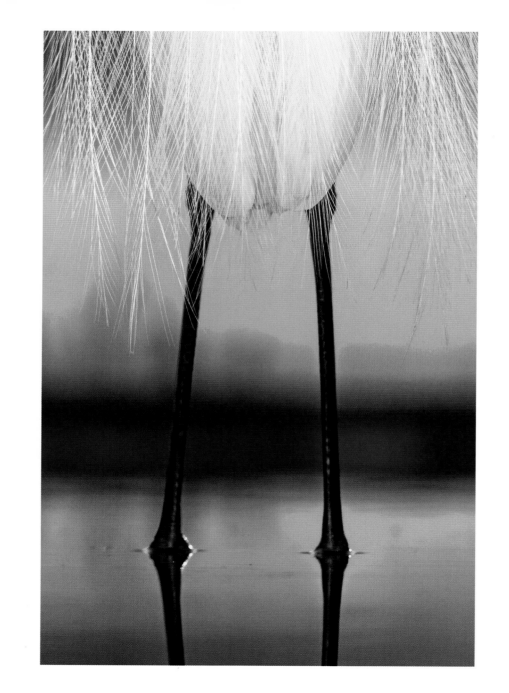

September

18 Monday

19 Tuesday

20 Wednesday

21 Thursday

22 Friday

| 23 Saturday | Autumn Equinox | 24 Sunday | Yom Kippur (Jewish) begins in the evening |

Dressed for dawn by Csaba Tökölyi
Csaba had been in a hide all night in Pusztaszer Natural Reserve, Hungary, photographing nocturnal species, but as the golden light of dawn reflected on the surface of the water, an egret in breeding plumage appeared. The elongated scapular feathers covered the bird as if it was wearing a gown.

September – October

25 Monday

Yom Kippur (Jewish)
ends in the evening

26 Tuesday

27 Wednesday

28 Thursday

29 Friday

30 Saturday

1 Sunday

What a poser by Clement Kiragu
In Kenya's Maasai Mara National Reserve, Clement spent time observing this
beautiful leopard as she soaked up the last warm rays of the setting sun. He
is mindful to take pleasure in life's simple moments, knowing that sometimes,
you can miss the exceptional while looking for the unusual.

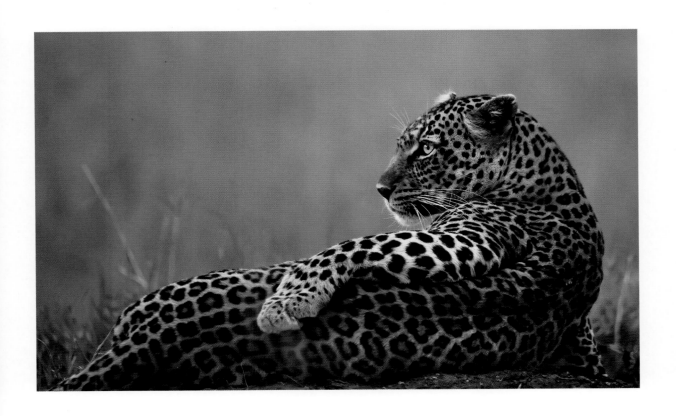

October

2 Monday

3 Tuesday

4 Wednesday

5 Thursday

6 Friday

7 Saturday

8 Sunday

The aquabatic antelope by Branson Meaker
Branson had spent hours trying to photograph the red lechwe on the flooded plains of Botswana's Kwando Reserve but the slightest noise, including the camera's shutter, spooked the shy animals. It was at sunset that he got the action shot he was after – a male leaping into the air.

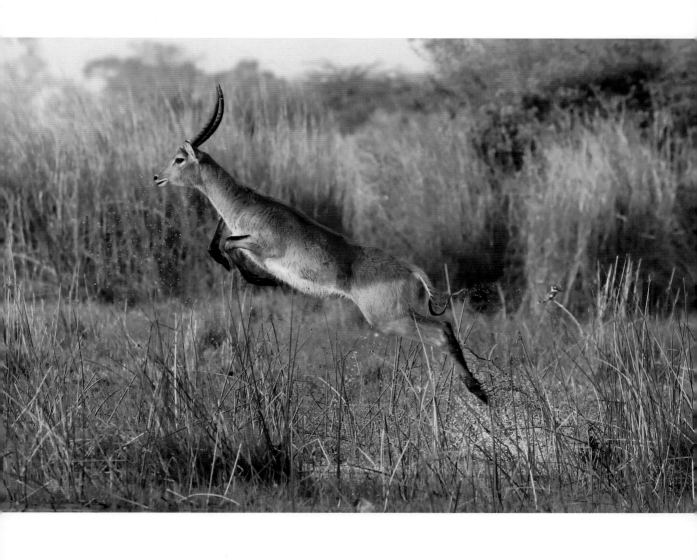

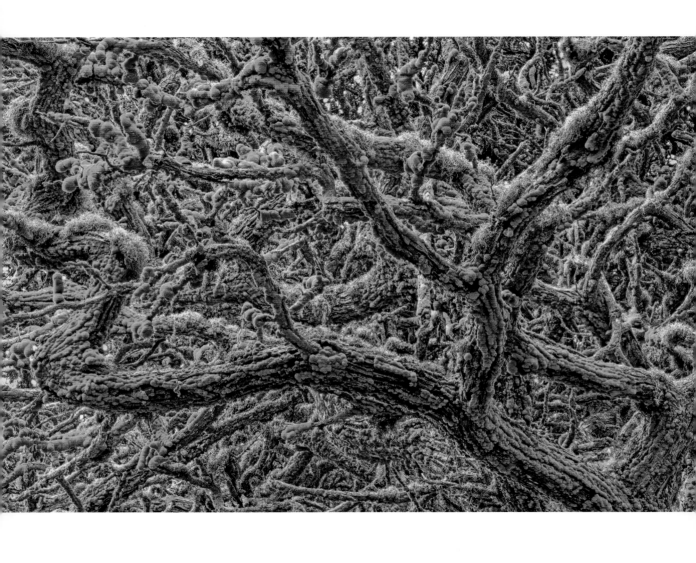

October

9 Monday

10 Tuesday

11 Wednesday

12 Thursday

13 Friday

14 Saturday

15 Sunday

Tapestry of life by Zorica Kovacevic
Festooned with bulging orange algae and grey lichen, the arms of a
Monterey cypress tree weave an otherworldly canopy over Pinnacle Point,
California, USA. This tiny, protected coastal zone is the only place in the
world where natural conditions combine to conjure this magical scene.

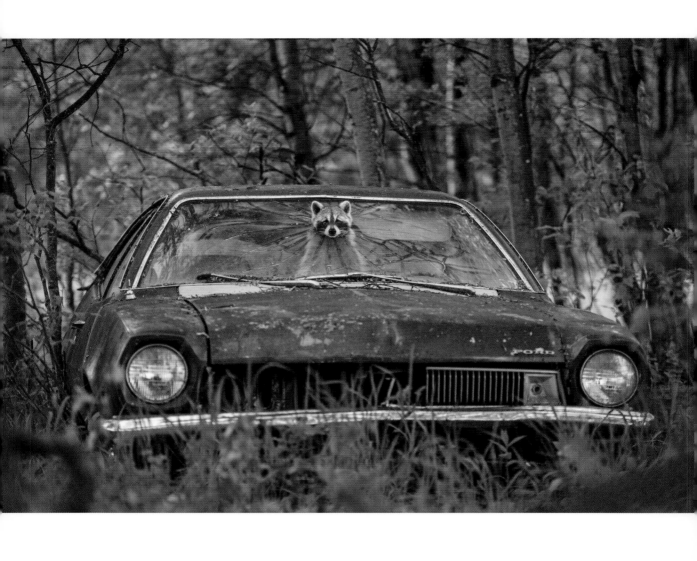

October

---

16 Monday

---

17 Tuesday

---

18 Wednesday

---

19 Thursday

---

20 Friday

---

21 Saturday	**22** Sunday

Lucky break by Jason Bantle
A raccoon pokes her bandit-masked face out of an abandoned car on a
deserted farm in Saskatchewan, Canada. In the back seat are her five playful
kits. On this evening, she paused at the exit just long enough for Jason to
take this picture, before squeezing out to spend the night looking for food.

October

---

23 Monday   Labour Day (New Zealand)

---

24 Tuesday

---

25 Wednesday

---

26 Thursday

---

27 Friday

---

28 Saturday | **29 Sunday**   British Summertime ends,
                                                                        clocks go back

---

The climbing dead by Frank Deschandol
On a fieldtrip in the Peruvian Amazon rainforest, Frank spotted this bizarre-
looking weevil clinging to a fern stem. Its glazed eyes showed that it was
dead, and the three antenna-like projections growing out of its thorax were
the ripe fruiting bodies of a parasitizing zombie fungus.

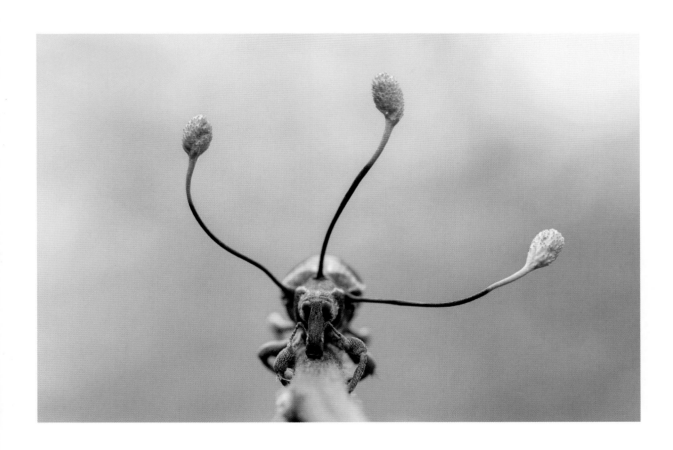

30 Monday

October holiday (Republic of Ireland)

31 Tuesday

Hallowe'en

1 Wednesday

All Saints' Day (Christian)

2 Thursday

3 Friday

4 Saturday

5 Sunday

Guy Fawkes/Bonfire Night (UK)

Jelly baby by Fabien Michenet
With nowhere to hide in the open ocean, a young jackfish adopts a small
jellyfish as shelter off Tahiti, French Polynesia. Fabien's speciality is diving in
deep open water, 'there is so much activity beneath the surface,' he says, and
in hundreds of nights dives has 'never seen one without the other'.

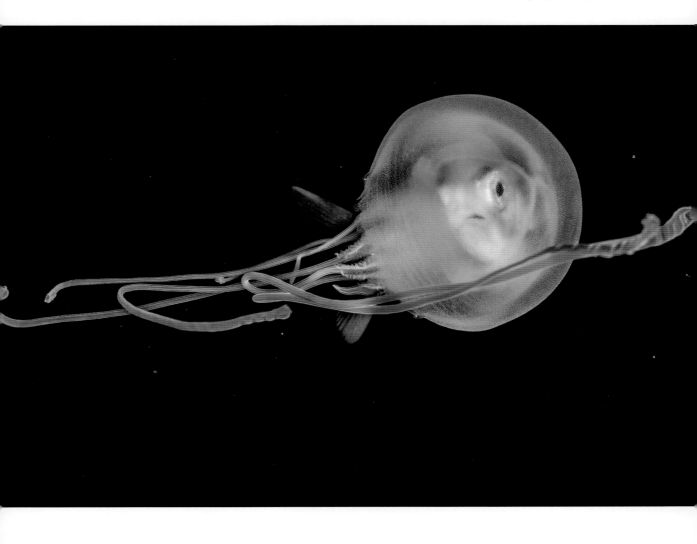

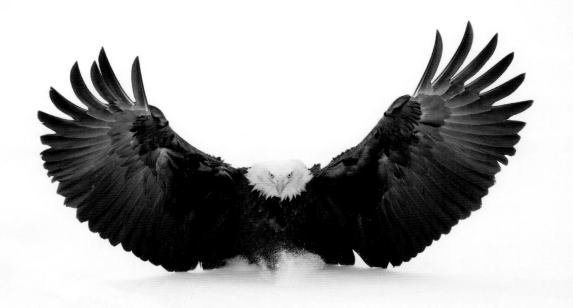

6 Monday

---

7 Tuesday

---

8 Wednesday

---

9 Thursday

---

10 Friday

| 11 Saturday | Armistice Day | 12 Sunday | Remembrance Sunday
Diwali (Sikh, Hindu) |

Snow landing by Jérémie Villet
With outstretched wings and instense eyes, a bald eagle lands in fresh snow
on the bank of a river in southeast Alaska. Its aim, to grab salmon from the
icy water below. Jérémie spent a week observing the behaviour of these
birds from a hide, and was well-positioned to capture this portrait.

November

13 Monday

14 Tuesday

15 Wednesday

16 Thursday

17 Friday

18 Saturday

19 Sunday

Teamwork by Jake Davis
Jake was on a boat off the coast of Great Bear Rainforest, British Columbia,
Canada, where he watched humpback whales bubble-net feeding. Here the
lead whale dives to locate the fish. Once located, the rest of the pod swim
in decreasing circles, blowing bubbles to create a net and trap the fish.

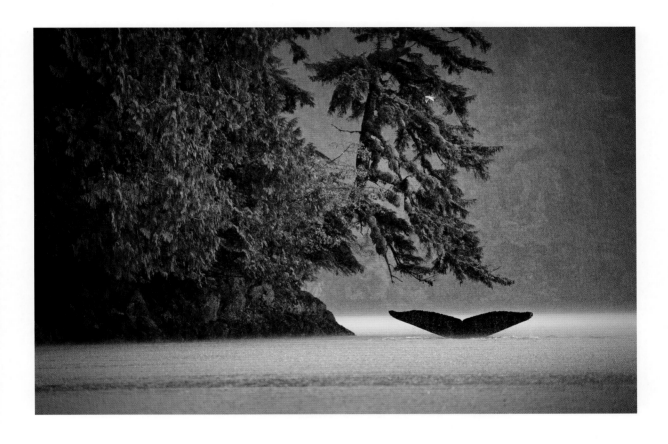

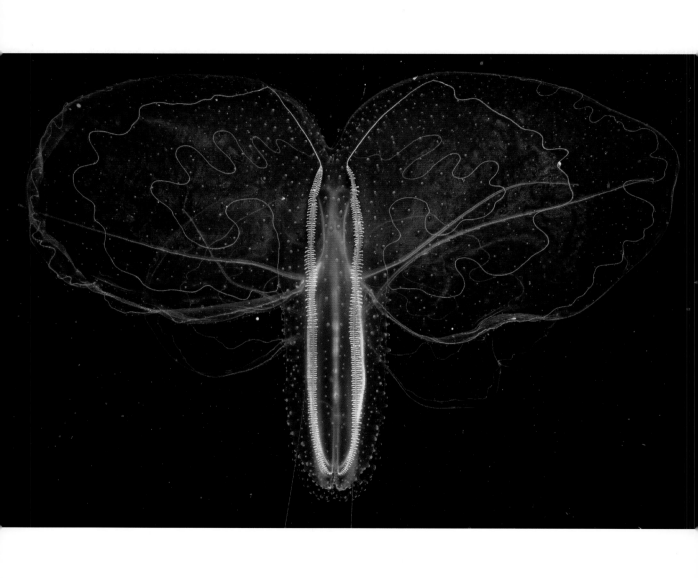

November

20 Monday

21 Tuesday

22 Wednesday

23 Thursday   Thanksgiving (USA)

24 Friday

25 Saturday

26 Sunday

The ethereal drifter by Angel Fitor
A delicate, transparent comb jelly stretches out its glassy sails as it rides the
Mediterranean currents trawling for food. Angel came across this pristine
individual on a dive 11 km (7 miles) off the coast of Alicante, Spain. Its
apparent blue colour is a product of the reflection of light from above.

27 Monday

28 Tuesday

29 Wednesday

30 Thursday   St Andrew's Day, holiday (Scotland)

1 Friday

2 Saturday

3 Sunday

One foggy night by Tamás Koncz-Bisztricz
On a late foggy November afternoon, in a forest near his home in southern
Hungary, Tamas noticed a familiar oak tree had taken on a new form against
the dusk sky. Using his camera's built-in flash, the fog surrounding the tree
transformed into a blizzard of sparkling water droplets.

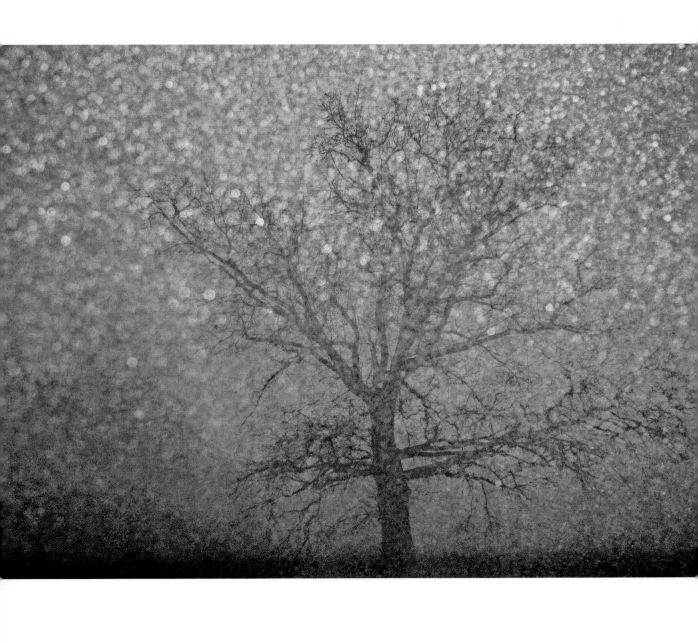

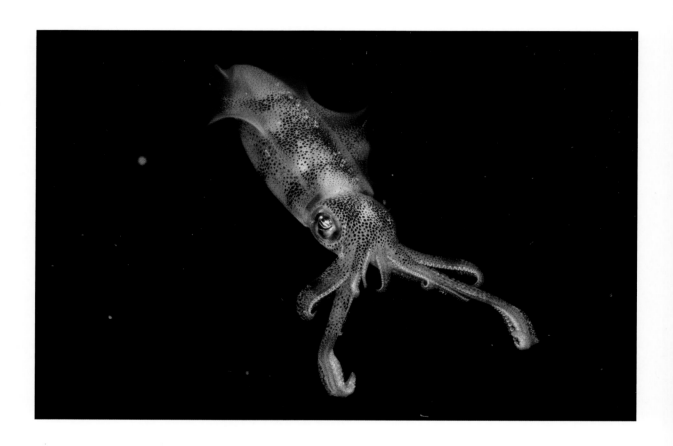

December

4 Monday

5 Tuesday

6 Wednesday

7 Thursday

Hanukkah, Festival of Lights (Jewish)
begins in the evening

8 Friday

9 Saturday

10 Sunday

Night glow by Cruz Erdmann
On a night dive in the Lembeh Strait off North Sulawesi, Indonesia, Cruz
chanced upon a pair of bigfin reef squid. They were engaged in a dazzling
courtship of changing colours and patterns. One jetted away, but the other
hovered just long enough for Cruz to capture its glowing underwater show.

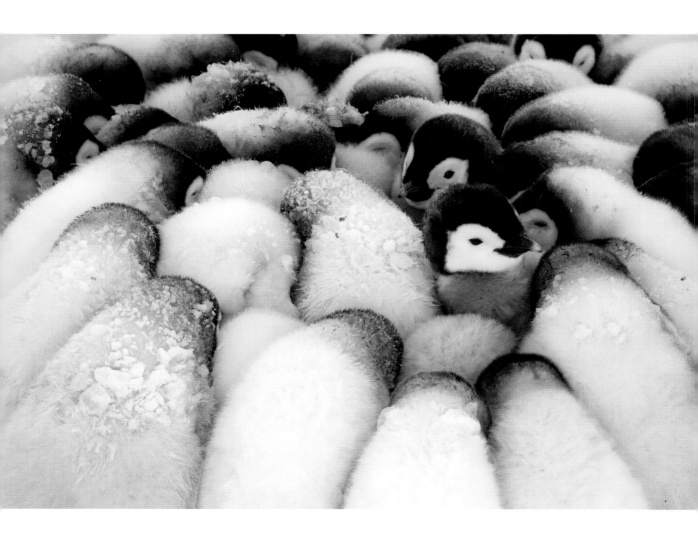

11 Monday

12 Tuesday

13 Wednesday

14 Thursday

15 Friday

Hanukkah, Festival of Lights (Jewish)
ends in the evening

16 Saturday

17 Sunday

Fluff formation by Stefan Christmann
'A few chicks started sticking their heads together,' says Stefan, 'and within minutes there was a fluff ball of about 50'. Unlike the vast huddles of adult emperor pengiuns, when the Antarctic temperatures drop or the wind picks up, mini huddles of fluff balls like this are spontaneous and disorderly.

December

WEEK 51

18 Monday

19 Tuesday

20 Wednesday

21 Thursday

22 Friday — Winter Solstice

23 Saturday

24 Sunday — Christmas Eve (Christian)

Tender play by Steve Levi
After 10 days of looking, Steve spotted this mother polar bear and her two cubs in early March. They had recently left their birthing den in Wapusk National Park, Canada, to begin the long journey to the sea ice so their mother could feed. After a nap the cubs were in a playful mood.

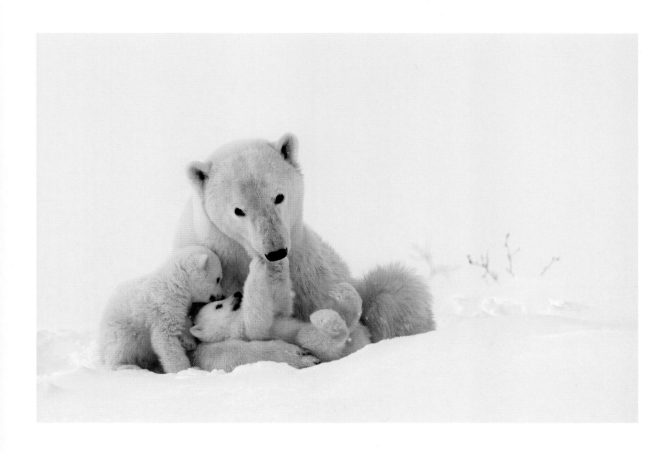

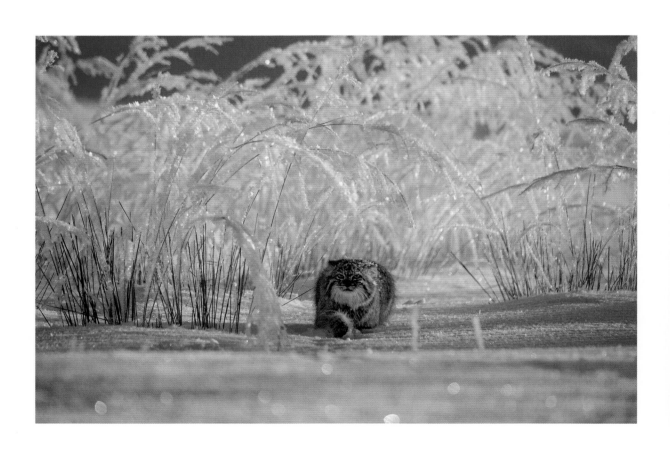

December

25 Monday   Christmas Day, holiday (Christian)

26 Tuesday   Boxing Day, holiday (Christian)

27 Wednesday

28 Thursday

29 Friday

30 Saturday

31 Sunday   New Year's Eve
                                                  Hogmanay (Scotland)

Winter's tale by Valeriy Maleev
Valeriy encountered this Pallas's cat while it was out hunting in the
Mongolian grasslands – it was -42˚C (-44˚F) on that frosty day, but the fairy
tale scene cancelled out the cold. Pallas's cats are no bigger than a domestic
cat and they stalk small rodents, birds and occasionally insects.

Notes

Notes

Index of photographers

Week 21
Trustful
Ingo Arndt
Germany
www.ingoarndt.com
Canon EOS 1D X Mark II + 600mm f4 lens + 2x extender; 1/750 sec at f8; ISO 2500; Gitzo tripod.

Week 37
Portrait of a mother
Ingo Arndt
Canon EOS-1D X Mark II + 600mm f4 lens + 1.4x extender; 1/1500 sec at f5.6; ISO 1000; Gitzo tripod.

Week 42
Lucky break
Jason Bantle
Canada
www.allinthewild.com
Nikon D810 + 70–200mm f2.8 lens at 145mm + polarizing filter; 0.4 sec at f2.8 (-0.7 e/v); ISO 800; cable release; Gitzo tripod + Wimberley head; hide.

Week 12
Dinner for one
Ripan Biswas
India
www.ripanbiswas.com
Nikon D500 + 18–55mm lens (reverse mounted); 1/125 sec; ISO 125; Godox V860II flash.

Week 25
Summer cornfield
Joël Brunet
France
www.joëlbrunet.com
Canon EOS 5D Mark IV + Sigma 120–300mm f2.8 lens at 180mm; 1/30 sec at f25; ISO 100.

Week 52 (2022)
Training session
Stefan Christmann
Germany
www.nature-in-focus.de
Nikon D810 + Nikon AF-S Nikkor 400mm f2.8 E FL ED VR lens; 1/1000 sec at f4.0; ISO 800.

Week 50
Fluff formation
Stefan Christmann
Nikon D700 + 70–200mm f2.8 lens at 195mm; 1/60 sec at f8; ISO 400.

Week 33
Beak to beak
Claudio Contreras Koob
Mexico
www.sulazul.com
Canon EOS 5D Mark II + Canon 300mm f2.8 Lens + Canon 2X Teleconverter II; 1/160 sec at f11; ISO 1600; Camo throwover blind.

Week 26
A bite to eat
Jaime Culebras
Spain
www.photowildlifetours.com
Canon EOS 6D + 100mm f2.8 lens; 1/100 sec at f16; ISO 200; Yongnuo flash + trigger; softbox.

Week 46
Teamwork
Jake Davis
USA
jakedavis@revealedinnature.com
Canon EOS 1D X Mark II + 100-400mm lens; 1/500 sec at f5.6; ISO 2500.

Week 32
Bee line
Frank Deschandol
France
www.frank-deschandol.com
Canon EOS 7D Mark II; 300mm f4 lens; 1/640 sec at f4; ISO 200.

Week 43
The climbing dead
Frank Deschandol
Canon EOS 5D Mark II + 100mm f2.8 lens; 1 sec at f5.6; ISO 100; Triopo tripod + Feisol head.

Week 30
A pulsing sea
David Doubilet
USA
www.daviddoubilet.com
Nikon D3S with Nikon 17-35mm f/28 lens in SEACAM Underwater housing. Sea & Sea YS 250 strobes at 1/2 power 1/50th sec f/10 at ISO 250.

Week 24
Humming surprise
Thomas Easterbrook
UK
stewart_easterbrook@hotmail.com
Sony DSC-HX400V + 24–210mm f2.8–6.3 lens at 51mm; 1/320 sec at f5; ISO 80

Week 49
Night glow
Cruz Erdmann
New Zealand
arnazmehta@gmail.com
Canon EOS 5D Mark III + 100mm f2.8 lens; 1/125 sec at f29; ISO 200; Ikelite DS161 strobe.

Week 35
The charm of Ruthy
Ariel Fields
Israel
www.arielfields.com
Nikon D500 + 200–500mm f5.6 lens at 500mm; 1/500 sec at f5.6 (-1 e/v); ISO 640.

Week 47
The ethereal drifter
Angel Fitor
Spain
www.seaframes.com
Nikon D800 + Sigma 20mm f1.8 lens; 1/250 sec at f16; ISO 50; Nexus housing; two Retra strobes.

Week 14
Forest refuge
Uge Fuertes Sanz
Spain
www.ugefuertes.com
Canon EOS 5D Mark III + 17–40mm f4 lens at 19mm; 1/80 sec at f13; ISO 640.

Week 15
Night rider
Wayne Jones
Australia
wjemptiness2@hotmail.com
Canon EOS 5D Mark IV + Sigma 70mm f2.8 Macro Art lens;1/200 sec at f16; ISO 400; Nauticam housing; two Retra UWT strobes + two Scubalamp RD90 spotting lights + two Weefine Smart Focus 3000 lights + four Scubalamp V6K Pro video lights + two Weefine Solar Flare Max video lights + two Divepro G18 Plus video lights.

Week 11
The white cliffs of Iturup
Alexey Kharitonov
Russia
www.facebook.com/akharitonoff
DJI Mavic Pro + 26mm f2.2 lens; 1/3200 sec at f2.2; ISO 100.

Cover & week 39
What a poser
Clement Kiragu
Kenya
www.clementwild.com
Canon EOS 5D Mark III + Sigma 150-500mm lens; 1/320 sec at f6.3; ISO 1250.

Week 48
One foggy night
Tamás Koncz-Bisztricz
Hungary
www.kbtamas.blogspot.com
Nikon COOLPIX P900; 1/30 sec at f2.8; ISO 400; built-in flash; Manfrotto tripod.

Week 41
Tapestry of life
Zorica Kovacevic
Serbia/USA
@zorica_kovacevic_beba
Nikon D850 + 70–200mm f2.8 lens at 112mm; 1/4 sec at f8; ISO 64; Really Right Stuff tripod + ballhead.

Week 51
Tender play
Steve Levi
USA
www.leviimages.com
Nikon D850 + 800mm f5.6 lens + 1.25x teleconverter at 1000mm; 1/1250 sec at f10; ISO 640.

Week 29
Meadow beauty
Alfons Lilja
Sweden
alfonslilja@gmail.com
Nikon D500 + 300mm f4 lens; 1/640 sec at f6.3; ISO 400.

Week 31
Big ears
Valeriy Maleev
Russia
facebook.com/valeriymaleev
Nikon D700 + Tamron Macro 1:1 90mm 1:2.8 lens; 1/400 sec at f5.6.

Week 52
Winter's tale
Valeriy Maleev
Nikon D4 + 80-400mm lens; 1/1000 sec at f7.1; ISO 1250.

Week 23
Early riser
Riccardo Marchegiani
Italy
www.joyoflight.it
Nikon D800E + 16–35mm f4 lens at 30mm; 1/60 sec at f8; ISO 100; Godox V860II-N flash.

Week 22
Lake of a million birds
Paul Mckenzie
Ireland
www.wildencounters.net
Canon EOS 5D Mark IV + 24–105mm f4 lens at 97mm; 1/8000 sec at f4; ISO 250.

Week 40
The aquabatic antelope
Branson Meaker
South Africa
www.bransonmeaker.com
Canon EOS 5D Mark III + 100–400mm f4.5–5.6 lens at 400mm; 1/2000 sec at f8; ISO 2000.

Week 44
Jelly baby
Fabien Michenet
France
www.fabienmichenet.photoshelter.com
Nikon D810 + 60mm f2.8 lens; 1/320 sec at f22; ISO 64; Nauticam housing; Inon Z-240 strobes.

Week 27
A swirl of rays
Duncan Murrell
UK
www.duncanmurrell.com
Canon EOS 6D + 15mm f2.8 fisheye lens; 1/200 sec at f7.1; ISO 500; Inon X-2 housing.

Week 8
The humpback calf
Wayne Osborn
Australia
www.wayneosborn.online
Canon EOS 5D Mark IV + EF 16-35mm f2.8 III USM Lens at 23mm; 1/200 sec at f8; ISO 320; Nauticam underwater housing with Zen 230mm Superdome.

Week 19
Dinner duty
Tommy Pedersen
Sweden
www.tommypedersen.se
Nikon D5 + 600mm f4 lens; 1/200 sec at f4.5; ISO 640; Gitzo tripod + Wimberley gimbal head.

Week 36
The plumage parade
Thomas P Peschak
Germany/South Africa
www.thomaspeschak.com
Nikon D5 + 24–70mm f2.8 lens at 24mm; 1/200 sec at f18; ISO 640; Profoto B1 flash.

Week 10
Spring vision
Imre Potyó
Hungary
www.facebook.com/imre.potyo
poimre@gmail.com
Nikon D90 + 50mm f1.8 lens + extension tube; 1/640 sec at f1.8; ISO 250.

Week 13
Great cormorant dry-off
Soumil Rathi
India
drshonalirathi@gmail.com
Canon EOS 700D + 250mm f4–5.6 lens; 1/320 sec at f7.1; ISO 100.

Week 4
Inquisitive
Audun Rikardsen
Norway
www.audunrikardsen.com
Canon 6D Mark II + Canon 8-15mm f4 lens; 1/640 sec at f18 (-1e/v); ISO 400, Canon 600II Flash; Siuri tripod head; motion sensor.

Week 18
The freshwater forest
Michel Roggo
Switzerland
www.roggo.ch
Sony 7R + 16–35mm f4 lens at 16mm; 1/40 sec at f8; ISO 200; Nauticam housing.

Week 1 (2023)
Sleeping like a Weddell
Ralf Schneider
Germany
www.raschphotography.com
Canon EOS 7D Mark II + 100–400mm f4.5–5.6 lens at 400mm; 1/500 sec at f8; ISO 400.

Week 2
Family get-together
Michael Schober
Austria
www.fotoschober.at
Nikon D4 + Nikon 17-35mm f2.8 lens; 640 sec; ISO 400.

Week 38
Dressed for dawn
Csaba Tökölyi
Hungary
www.csabatokolyi.com
Nikon D7200 + Nikon 300mm f2.8 AF-S VR lens; 1/640 sec at f7.1; ISO 1600; hide.

Week 28
War dance
Victor Tyakht
Russia
www.sfdp.ru/victortyakht
Sony RX10 IV + Zeiss Vario-Sonnar 8.8–220mm f2.4–4 lens; 1/2000 sec at f6.3; ISO 400.

Week 16
A suitable gift
Marco Valentini
Italy
www.pbase.com/marcovalentini
Canon 5D Mark III + Canon 500 IS ii lens; 1/640 sec at f.8; ISO 500.

Week 3
Snow hunting
Jérémie Villet
France
www.instagram.com/jeremievillet
Canon EOS 7D Mark II + 400mm f2.8 lens; 1/6400 sec at f4.5 (+0.7 e/v); ISO 500.

Week 7
Frozen moment
Jérémie Villet
Canon EOS 5D Mark IV + 400mm f2.8 lens; 1/1600 sec at f2.8 (+1.3 e/v); ISO 500.

Week 45
Snow landing
Jérémie Villet
Canon EOS 5D Mark IV + 400mm f2.8 lens; 1/3200 sec at f4; ISO 1600.

Week 17
Mother knows best
Marion Vollborn
Germany
www.tierundnaturfoto.de
Canon EOS 1D X + EF70-200mm f2.8L IS II USM lens; 1/640 sec at f4.5 (-0.33e/v); ISO 3200.

Week 5
Snow exposure
Max Waugh
USA
www.maxwaugh.com
Canon EOS-1D X + 100–400mm f5.6 lens at 200mm; 1/15 sec at f22 (+1 e/v); ISO 100.

Week 34
The hair-net cocoon
Minghui Yuan
China
ymh2zml@163.com
Nikon D500 + 85mm f3.5 lens; 1/50 sec at f29 (+2 e/v); ISO 640.

Week 20
Sky hole
Sven Zacek
Estonia
www.zacekfoto.ee
DJI Phantom 4 Pro + 8.8mm lens; 1/100 sec at f4.5; ISO 100.

Week 6
The frozen spires
Roberto Zanette
Italy
robertozanette@hotmail.it
Nikon D3S + 80–200mm f2.8 lens at 155mm + polarizing filter; 1/400 sec at f8; ISO 200.

Week 9
Matching outfits
Michel Zoghzoghi
Lebanon
@michel_zoghzoghi
Canon EOS 1D X Mark II +500mm f4 lens; 1/1250 sec at f13 (-1e/v); ISO 1250.

First published by the Natural History Museum, Cromwell Road, London SW7 5BD.
© The Trustees of the Natural History Museum, London 2022. All Rights Reserved.
Photographs © the individual photographers.
Text based on original captions used in the Wildlife Photographer of the Year exhibitions.
ISBN: 978 0 565 09530 7
All rights reserved. No part of this publication may be transmitted in any form or by any means without prior permission of the publisher.
A catalogue record for this book is available from the British Library.
Printed by Toppan Leefung Printing Ltd. China.

Every effort has been made to ensure the accuracy of listed holiday dates, however, some may have changed after publication for official or cultural reasons.